LAY IT ON ME

PERRY STONE, JR.

LAY IT ON ME

PERRY STONE, JR.

Published by

Voice of Evangelism Outreach Ministries

Unless otherwise indicated, all scripture quotations are taken from the *New King James Version* of the Bible.

Lay It On Me
By Perry Stone, Jr.

Voice of Evangelism Outreach Ministries, Inc.
All rights reserved
P.O. Box 3595
Cleveland, Tennessee 37320
www.perrystone.org

Printed by Modern Way Printing and Fulfillment
Ooltewah, TN 37363

Printed in the United States of America

Contents

THE RUTH IN MY LIFE

Once there were three little girls. Each had her own unique personality, beauty and dreams. As they grew, unexpected difficulties came into their lives. When the three were teenagers, their parents separated and divorced, inflicting great sorrow and pain on these tender young women.

Not long after that misfortune, a dear loved one experienced an emotional breakdown. Instead of blaming God and becoming bitter about these unfortunate family circumstances, all the girls held on to their faith. They continued to sing in the church choir and attend prayer meetings and revivals.

They had the spirit of Ruth—they were always ready to serve.

One, in particular, would babysit the children and help cook the evening meals for the church family who had taken in her and her two sisters. Here she was, a *stranger* in the house of another family; yet, she continued to cook, clean house, babysit and minister to the needs of those around her. She sought no compensation.

This quiet little girl became a young woman with a strong faith in God. Her name is *Pamela*, which means "sweet as honey."

During a four-week revival in Northport, Alabama, I discovered her, my "Ruth," sitting on a corner pew with other young people, weeping and worshiping God. Even in the midst of several hundred people, this beautiful young woman stood out. Her beautiful complexion and her long brunette hair, curled at the end, first caught my eye. Her pretty green eyes hypnotized me. And that smile—she had a smile that would make any single young man look twice! Her gentle spirit wooed me.

On April 2, 1982, I was the most honored man in the world, as I walked this young lady down the aisle of her home church and took her to be my wife.

Pam, when I read the Book of Ruth, I think of you. There are many parallels between you and this woman of destiny. You left friends, family and everything close to you in order to follow me into the harvest field. You have labored with me for many years without complaint. You were a virgin when we married and have remained a virtuous woman to this day.

You and I are a team. We have gone from small beginnings to a world-wide ministry. I owe so much of my success to my little "Ruth." You are my right arm!

Pammy, I am dedicating this book to you. Hidden in its pages is the pattern of your life. I feel like your little "Boaz." I am honored to have you "spread your skirt over my feet" and cuddle next to me until the sun rises in the morning.

People who know you, know well the character you display and the commitment you carry for the work of God. I know of no woman alive who could do what you do and be such a blessing to the ministry. You are one of a kind.

PREFACE

The story of Ruth has all the elements of a giant box-office hit. It contains sudden trouble, tragedy and death. It has romance, love and success. It is a rags-to-riches story. The difference, however, is that it is not fiction. It has endured through time as one of the greatest stories in the Bible.

The Book of Ruth contains only four chapters. Yet, this powerful story provides spiritual principles of how to progress in the blessings of God, and how grace and favor work on your behalf.

This exciting adventure story gives you hope. It is a hope that no matter what you encounter in life, whether it is famine, death or lack, God has a grand finale planned for your life! It shows that God is sovereign, even in death. God is planning a long-term blessing for you, even when things look the darkest.

This truth reminds me of what the writer said in Hebrews 10:9: "He takes away the first that He may establish the second." You will learn, in reading this book, that God never allows you to lose anything unless He plans to return something better than what you had.

Your reaction to trouble will determine your outcome.

Experiencing tragedy and trials is never easy. Several times I have wanted to give up and get a "normal job." At other times I have wanted to resign my position and go to work for another ministry. Then, at least, I would not have to shoulder the heavy load of directing a ministry. During those times, God reminds me of where I have been and from where He has brought me.

Like the psalmist David, I muse on the wonderful works of the Lord (Psalm 39:3)! In an unexpected moment, I receive a renewing of the vision that enables me to continue "across the Jordan" to take possession of the promises of God!

God has brought our ministry from a local church ministry, preaching to 20 people a night, to an international ministry, reaching millions in both North America and in foreign lands. The spiritual truths and Kingdom keys found in the story of Ruth are the same truths that have carried our ministry from one level to the next.

As you read this book, may your inner man receive the same revelation I did. May that revelation move you into the progression of the blessings of the Lord! You will be ready for God to *Lay It On You!*

Chapter 1

When the Unexpected Happens

Much can change in 24 hours. Decisions you make today can affect your life forever. Many choices we make are based on a preconceived idea of an expected outcome. We flee conflict and cling to success. To us, it seems impossible that a good God could allow bad things to happen to good people. Jesus said, however, "your Father in heaven . . . sends rain on the just and on the unjust" (Matthew 5:45).

Some foundations melt under the pressure of storms because the house was not built on the Rock, Christ Jesus. Others can experience the same trouble, stand dripping wet amid deafening thunder and blinding lightning and yet still remain firm when the clouds of darkness have lifted to reveal the much-needed sun. The difference is who or what you are trusting and how you react to trouble. The Book of Ruth gives us insight into how people should and should not react when the unexpected happens.

This story begins with famine and death. In an effort to flee a terrible famine, Elimelech and his family migrated to Moab. While there, he and his two sons, both of whom had taken Moabite women for wives, died. As if the devastating feeling of lack was not enough, now Naomi, Orpah and Ruth were widows. Want and separation consumed the lives of the three widows left to carry on in Moab.

Tragedies, such as famine and death, move people either closer to God or further from Him. Naomi, for example, was a strong woman who, instead of being broken, became resentful. Yet, the same set of circumstances that brought Ruth into the family would also produce the royal lineage of Israel.

When Naomi and her husband fled with their two sons to escape the famine in Judah, she never knew that 10 years later she would return, a broken, depressed and bitter woman. Who did she feel was responsible for this? Naomi revealed this when she said, "The Almighty has dealt very bitterly with me" (Ruth 1:20). Tragedy had caused her to lose her vision, her purpose and her concept of God.

Famine can test your faith and resolve, and death can separate you not only from the one you love, but can separate your faith from the giver of life. Too often we blame God for every tragedy that happens.

Life, once sweet, can suddenly turn painful. The same sun that melts wax, hardens clay. The victories of today can turn into the sorrows of tomorrow. But if we open our hearts to the story of Ruth, we can understand how God plans His long-term purpose in the midst of trouble. We can understand how we may better deal with these unexpected turns in life.

FAMINE IN STRANGE PLACES

Throughout the Bible, Bethlehem is a special city. Rachel, a matriarch who died in childbirth, was laid to rest on the outskirts of this city (Genesis 35:16-20). So, from its earliest days, this small village has been associated with death and separation. Yet, the name *Bethlehem* implies blessing. It comes from two Hebrew words, *beyth* which means "house," and *lechem* which means "bread."

Bethlehem was known for its large fields, which were divided into sections. Here, farmers would harvest barley in the mid to late spring, and wheat in the summer. The grain used to make the bread for the table of shewbread was taken from the fields of Bethlehem. It seems odd that the "house of bread" would experience lack, especially a famine.

Famines are caused by droughts which, in turn, are caused by a lack of rain. In a spiritual application, spiritual famines are caused by a lack of spiritual rain. When the Holy Spirit is not being poured out in churches, a spiritual famine occurs. There is a famine in the world today—not of bread, but of the Word.

People will eat the strangest things in times of famine. When people get hungry, this causes their flesh to begin to react in strange ways. In one instance, mothers were eating their children during a severe famine (2 Kings 6:28, 29). Likewise, when a church becomes dry and stagnant, the people begin to turn on one another. Soon gossip and backbiting become commonplace. In Paul's words, "You bite and devour one another" (Galatians 5:15).

Numbers 11 reveals that the Hebrews grew tired of manna and began to complain. The taste of Egypt was still in their mouths. "Who will give us meat to eat?" they asked (Numbers 11:4). To appease the grumblers, God sent quail that accumulated three feet deep in the desert (Numbers 11:31)! God allowed them to gorge their flesh by eating flesh. After a period of time, judgment fell and the flesh eaters died in the wilderness (Numbers 11:33).

When believers devour one another with cutting words, the entire body of Christ is affected. When people use harsh words to cut and destroy people, the result will be physical sickness. Paul wrote to the Corinthian church and addressed the division and strife among them. Paul revealed:

> For he who eats and drinks in an unworthy manner eats and drinks judgment to himself, not discerning the Lord's body. For this reason many are weak and sick among you, and many sleep (1 Corinthians 11:29, 30).

During severe droughts and famines, humans have not only devoured other humans, but things a person would never eat suddenly become appetizing! During a famine in 2 Kings 6:25, people were selling dove's dung and donkey brains in order to survive. Starving people will do just about anything!

When famine hit Bethlehem, one Jewish family made an unusual move. They crossed the Jordan River into the land of the Moabites. For Elimelech, a Jew, and his family to live in Moab was an unusual occurrence. The Moabites were descendants of an incestuous relationship between Lot and one of his daughters. In fact, the Moabites were placed under a curse by the Law of Moses (Deuteronomy 23:2-4).

So for Elimelech and his family to leave Bethlehem and go to Moab was regression, not progression. But when people are hungry, they will look for bread in unusual places.

UNEXPECTED TRAGEDY

While in Moab, Naomi's two sons, Mahlon and Chilion, married two Moabite women, Ruth and Orpah. We are uncertain what happened, but both sons died in Moab. Elimelech, Naomi's husband, also passed away. In ancient times there were no government social programs or financial assistance for widows. A woman losing her husband lost more than a companion; she also lost her financial security.

At this point, Naomi's future was in jeopardy. Normally, when a man passed away, his oldest son would inherit the property and the land. When Naomi's husband died, the inheritance left in Bethlehem was in danger of being claimed by other family members because her sons had also died. Unless something happened, she would lose it all. If she remained in a foreign land, she would have to relinquish all rights to her husband's land.

To have any chance at all of getting her property back, she would have to return to Bethlehem. Even then, she would not be able to retain the property for herself. One of her husband's kisman would have to step forward and redeem it for her. Naomi was practically destitute.

THE DANGER OF STAYING IN MOAB

As noted, the land of Moab was under a curse, according to the Law of Moses. A Moabite was not to enter the congregation of the Lord up to the 10th generation. The curse was caused because the Moabites were the descendants of an incestuous relationship between Lot and one of his daughters.

In order to break the curse, a Moabite had to convert to the God of Abraham, Isaac and Jacob. This meant they would have to leave their homeland and journey to a place they had never seen. Some were willing to break with everything they have ever known and cross the river of destiny. Most, however, continued on in Moab.

When Naomi decided to return to her home, her daughter-in-law, Orpah, decided to remain in Moab. Her choice was a decision to continue in her past. Orpah could sit on the mountainside overlooking Israel and see the hills of Bethlehem, but she never crossed the Jordan. Her life was a humdrum existence of memories of death, three funerals and a mother-in-law and a sister-in-law she would never see again.

Moab is a place of bad experiences and bad memories. In Moab, you're always living in the past. The country, Moab, was named after the son of Lot. When Lot fled Sodom with his two daughters, as far as they knew they were the only ones left on earth. The daughters, thinking this was the end of humanity, decided to get their father drunk and have sexual relations with him. This, they thought, would ensure that mankind would continue on.

As a result of this scheme, two sons were born. One was named Ben Ami, and he was the father of the Ammonites. The other was named Moab (Genesis 19:37, 38). As Lot watched Moab grow up, he was constantly tormented by his past. Moab was a living reminder of that terrible night in the cave when, in a drunken stupor, Lot begat a son by his own daughter.

In Moab, people are reminded of the "one-night-stands" that birthed the unexpected. Bad things happen in Moab. Three godly men died there. It is a place of sorrow. Linger in Moab, and you are reminded, repeatedly, of past failures, of the affair you had, of the time you backslid. Thoughts of tragedy and "what-if" haunt you. Moab represents events in your life you'd rather forget.

In Mark 5, the man of Gadara was possessed with 2,000 evil spirits (Mark 5). He lived among the tombs; he resided in a graveyard (Mark 5:3). A graveyard is a place of death. Dotting the landscape of a graveyard are headstones, macabre reminders of a person's past. You see, a graveyard has no future. A cemetery is simply a memorial to a life that used to be. When entering a graveyard, people who are still living spend most of their time weeping.

Into this kind of environment, the devil drove the man of Gadara. He was stranded in the wilderness, living among the ruins of the past. The Enemy wants you to stay in Moab. He wants to remind you of your failures. As long as you dwell in the tombs of yesterday you will not move toward a resurrection of hope in your tomorrows.

Day and night, the man in the tombs cried out in torment, (Mark 5:5). Do you have restless days and restless nights without relief? Do you cringe in the morning and the evening because your life is at a standstill? Perhaps you can "break chains," but you cannot get out of the graveyard. You have physical strength, but you are so tormented by the Enemy that he paralyzes your spirit.

The tomb is where memories are buried deep in the ground — memories of what could have been if things had turned out differently. Yet, everything around you is dead! Your marriage is dead, your family has no joy and your job is a burden. You are stuck in Moab, living among the tombs!

Moab is a real place. It is where bad things happen to good people. To come into the future blessings of God, you must make a break from Moab. Like the man from Gadara, you must have an encounter with Jesus and come out of the tombs! You must forget those things which are behind and reach forward to those things which are ahead (Philippians 3:13).

No doubt you will encounter obstacles. Moab and Bethlehem are separated by the Jordan River. It must be crossed. It will take faith to leave your past and head toward your future. It will take courage to cross the Jordan River and go into an area of work or ministry you have never known. Friends will tell you to stay where you are; but there comes a time when you must realize God has a divine connection for you in Bethlehem.

DEPRESSED PEOPLE
GIVE THE WRONG ADVICE

After all of her troubles in Moab, Naomi finally decided to return home. She would leave her past and go back to Bethlehem (Ruth 1:22). Instead of returning home joyously, however, she returned home devastated. Naomi was a strong woman who, instead of being broken, had become bitter.

Naomi's bitterness was obvious in her interaction with those who loved her. It appears that when Naomi began to leave Moab, both Ruth and Orpah decided to leave with her:

> THEREFORE SHE WENT OUT FROM THE PLACE WHERE SHE WAS, AND HER TWO DAUGHTERS-IN-LAW WITH HER; AND THEY WENT ON THE WAY TO RETURN TO THE LAND OF JUDAH. THEY SAID TO HER, "SURELY WE WILL RETURN WITH YOU TO YOUR PEOPLE" (RUTH 1:7, 10).

Three times Naomi discouraged the girls from going with her to Bethlehem (Ruth 1:8-13). In fact, the context seems to indicate that she was commanding them not to follow her. She commanded them to go back to Moab and find husbands among their own people. Why did Naomi discourage them? Because she was discouraged! In verse 20, Naomi revealed her emotional condition:

DO NOT CALL ME NAOMI; CALL ME MARA, FOR THE AL-MIGHTY HAS DEALT VERY BITTERLY WITH ME.

Naomi was bitter at God for the loss of her husband and two sons. She said, "The hand of the Lord has gone out against me" (Ruth 1:13)! The name "Mara" is a form of the word *marah*. In the wilderness, Israel came to the bitter waters of Marah and could not drink until the waters were sweetened. *Strongs Greek and Hebrew Bible Dictionary* says the word means "a bitter place in the desert."

When Moses threw wood into the bitter water of Marah, then the bitterness was made sweet. The Cross of Christ can still make bitter waters sweet!

Yet, Naomi had been through so much hurt that she wasn't able to encourage others who were hurting. One who is whole needs no physician (Matthew 9:12). It is possible for a healthy person to nurse someone else back to health, but a person who needs a doctor certainly cannot heal someone else. Likewise, a person who is hurting terribly has insufficient faith to heal another who is suffering. Bitter people make other bitter people more bitter. Angry people make other angry people angrier. Hurting people have difficulty in healing hurting people.

Apparently, Naomi had not prayed about God's will for Ruth and Orpah. Chances are she had not consulted the Lord about her own decision. When famine hit Bethlehem, why did her family move to Moab? Did they pray about it? They heard that bread was in Moab, and they responded. Now Naomi hears there is bread back home. It seems that the things Naomi heard always moved her. By examining Naomi's reaction to circumstances, we learn two valuable lessons.

> **FIRST, NEVER ASSUME THAT THE OBVIOUS THING IS THE RIGHT THING.** WE SHOULD ALWAYS SEEK TO KNOW WHAT GOD'S WILL IS IN ANY SITUATION.

> **SECOND, NEVER TAKE ADVICE FROM A BITTER PERSON.** THEY COULD GIVE YOU THE WRONG COUNSEL. THEIR THINKING IS BLURRED AND THEIR FAITH IS WEAK.

Naomi reasoned, *I cannot have any more sons. If I could, my daughters-in-law would be too old to marry them. Ruth and Orpah need to stay here.* Since Ruth and Orpah were familiar with the surroundings, Naomi wanted them to stay. Naomi wanted to enter Bethlehem alone in order to demonstrate how lonely and isolated her life had become.

As the story continued to unfold, however, the two young women make two completely different choices. Thank God, Ruth felt a connection with Naomi. Ruth remembered the joy when Mahlon, Naomi's son, was engaged to her. She recalled Naomi talking about a possible grandson, and describing how the wedding would be a giant celebration.

Ruth knew that Naomi needed healing. Ruth knew a little girl was locked up inside of this bitter woman. She knew that Naomi longed to have a grandchild bouncing on her knee. Ruth wanted to be a part of Naomi's life. She yearned to see Naomi the way she was before this triple tragedy struck in her life.

This factor distinguishes Ruth from Orpah. Orpah was selfish. She stayed in Moab, thinking, *If I stay here, I will find the right husband. God can bless me as well in Moab as He can in Bethlehem.* Ruth, however, thought of others. She was not looking for a husband, she wanted to meet a need. She believed the distress of one who needed a friend was more important than her own need for a husband. Ruth would not let Naomi walk alone.

Ruth saw the situation and sensed something special. She recognized the call to minister to someone. When most people receive a "call from God," most people interpret it as a call for their ministry or a call to use their gift.

By contrast, Ruth was called to someone else. It was a burden to move to Bethlehem. It would require her to leave her homeland. She would be separated from childhood friends and loving neighbors. It would mean she would have to walk on strange soil, among strange people with different beliefs and customs. She would live among the Jews, the covenant people of God!

Ruth must have known that Jews were suspicious of strangers. The young Moabite would have to prove herself. Still, she and Naomi had much in common. They were related through marriage. Both had experienced the death of their husbands, and both were leaving the past behind. Orpah, on the other hand, could not make the break.

Chapter 2

Daters and Romancers

THEN THEY LIFTED UP THEIR VOICES AND WEPT AGAIN; AND
ORPAH KISSED HER MOTHER-IN-LAW, BUT RUTH CLUNG TO
HER (RUTH 1:14).

Orpah kissed and Ruth clave (in the words of the authorized text.) This reveals the reaction of those who serve themselves, and those who serve others and the Lord. Some people serve you from a distance and tell you how much they appreciate the ministry or your work. They will gladly follow —*from a distance!*

Others will cleave to you because they have a burden for the work. Orpah was a woman of great words, but Ruth was a woman of great works.

The church consists, basically, of two groups—the kissers and the cleavers, or, as I will call them, the daters and the romancers. *The daters* show up at their own convenience and on their own time to let the Lord know they have "made their appearance" at His house. They "blow kisses" to the Lord for two hours on Sunday to let Him know, "I do love You. I may not be back for a few weeks, but I love You. I may not see You again for awhile, but I will have You on my mind."

Then there are the romancers. I learned years ago, before Pam and I were married, the difference between dating and romancing. Anyone can go on a date, but romance is a different story. Most men go on a date to get a kiss from the woman. A romancer takes her out and spoils her with flowers, cards, words of affection and attention. He opens door for her, sits in a candle-lit restaurant and holds her hand. Kissing is an act of the flesh, but romance is a thing of the heart.

When I courted my wife, I wanted to be near her just to hear her speak with the soft, southern, Alabama accent. Looking into her soft, green eyes and holding her hand was a thrill. Having her sitting next to me was the joy of my day. Before we were married, I often drove 10 hours one way, just to spend an entire day in the presence of this unique woman. Men who love God will go out of their way to find a Ruth.

If you are courting Him for His blessings, then you are just "dating God." When you are "romancing your Lover," then you hear an intimate song pouring from your spirit in praise to Him. You will run to your room and open His love letter, the Bible. When you play gospel music, a praise is birthed in your heart. If He never gave me another blessing, I would love just to feel His presence. Take my earthly possessions but don't take His presence.

When Orpah, the dater, kissed her mother-in-law goodbye, she bade farewell to her destiny. At the same moment, Ruth the romancer grabbed Naomi's garment and clung to her side, saying:

Wherever you go, I will go; and wherever you lodge, I will lodge; your people shall be my people, and your God, my God (Ruth 1:16).

How Much Do You Want It?

How much do you want God's perfect will and direction for your life? Do you want it enough to spend all night praying? Is it important enough for you to spend your evenings alone while others are out having a picnic or going to the theater? Do you desire His perfect will to the extent that you would pack up and go where you have never been before?

If necessary, would you leave home and the security of those you know just to minister to people you have never seen? Are you willing to leave your past behind in Moab? Are you willing to go into the new territory of Bethlehem? Are you willing to step out, as Abraham did, "going and not knowing?" How determined are you to do the will of God? You must remember that being in God's will can often be difficult and, at times, lonely.

In my early ministry, I spent five years traveling alone to towns I had never been in, staying in strange homes among unfamiliar people. I often had emotionally bad times because of bad experiences. I remember going to churches to preach revivals, only to discover that the meeting had not even been announced. Posters our office had sent in advance were discarded beneath the pulpit. In instances like this, often half the congregation stayed home the first night.

Knowledge begets confidence, and I knew that I was in God's will. Had I not known this, I would have fainted. There were many times when I felt like quitting and going back to Moab, defeated by discouragement. Yet, I knew God had called me.

DISCOURAGED BY FAMILY

At age 16, I announced to my family that I was called to preach. Nobody was excited but me. No one close to me really believed I was actually called to preach, and I knew why. Friends and family knew me too well. I loved sports. I "cut up" all the time. I was never serious about anything.

Granddad said I could have been a comedian. Most thought I was caught up in an emotional moment and after a sermon or two, my desire to preach would subside.

My father, who had been in ministry for over 45 years, did more than anyone to discourage me. About a month before I preached my first sermon in his church, Dad became very negative, telling me difficult and discouraging things about ministry. He never said an encouraging word to me.

Years later, I asked him why he was so negative. He said he knew if his words could discourage me, then I was never called to preach. If his discouragement did not deter me, however, then he felt I was truly called. Dad's insight and logic was correct.

When I asked my grandfather if I could come to his church in Gorman, Maryland, he thought I was coming to play the drums (I had played for eight years). When he realized I intended to preach, he couldn't believe it. I recall him saying, "I always thought Perry would end up being a comedian."

At 18 years of age, I entered a time of fasting and praying for personal direction. During this season of prayer, I went to the Virginia State Camp Meeting in Roanoke, Virginia. In that meeting, a respected minister asked me about my plans in ministry. When I told him, he said, "You will never amount to anything unless you follow the pattern of our denomination."

Years later, several ministers confessed that when I was a teenage preacher, they said among themselves, "He is full of wildfire, and it will soon blow over." Others bet on how long I would last before quitting. Still others felt that because I was ministering in extended revivals and seeing great spiritual results, I would succumb to pride, and fail in the ministry.

All of this negative attention began to take its toll. In fact, I lived under a cloud of depression for about three years. I have often wondered why I did not just give up and quit the ministry. If some had experienced the criticism and discouragements that I have, then they would have selected another occupation. After years of wondering how I made it through all that, I believe I have the answer.

Something within me was restless. That restlessness has never ceased. In 1976, when I was preaching to 15 people, I knew there was something more. I have since preached to 10,000 in just one service, and I still feel that there is more! When I witnessed the first soul converted under my ministry, I knew there was more.

I have since seen 3,000 saved in just one service. Early in the ministry, I was thrilled to see two Methodist ladies filled with the Holy Spirit. Now we see as many as 150 filled in a single service. Yet, I sense the time will come when 25,000 will receive the Holy Spirit baptism in one service!

Building for the Future

My restlessness tells me that I have not seen what God can and will do. It is divine discontent that moves you from your place of security and comfort, across the Jordan River, to a new territory, to new dreams and to new blessings.

When we first published the *Voice of Evangelism* magazine, it was a small, one-color flyer, full of spelling errors and typos. Yet, I did not despise a small beginning (Job 8:7). I continued to be faithful in the little things, despite the fact that for five years I received almost no response in the mail or financial assistance for the printing. I did it because a word from God burned within me.

I had been in Moab. I had been discouraged and laughed at. Some told me I was never called to preach. I attended the "school of the wilderness" for my early training. Like Ruth, I had a divine restlessness, and knew there was something more than what I was seeing. I had tasted the bread of Moab, and had a desire to taste the bread from Bethlehem.

When I came forth from the womb, yelling at the top of my lungs, I was born for this hour. The desire to pursue the things of God was, and is, burning within me! Knowing that God will use this mortal vessel provokes me to action. Crossing Jordan is a must, because my blessing is awaiting me. I have been in ministry over 28 years now, and continue to sense that I have still not realized my final destiny.

In 1989, I experienced a vision. In this vision I heard the voice of God say, "All I'm going to tell you now is Psalm 2:8." I awoke, ran downstairs and opened my Bible to read Psalm 2:8. What I found written there startled me:

ASK OF ME, AND I WILL GIVE YOU THE NATIONS FOR YOUR INHERITANCE, AND THE ENDS OF THE EARTH FOR YOUR POSSESSION.

It seemed the Lord was calling me to foreign nations! Yet, I had not preached overseas one time. I had not left Moab, but I knew I soon would. I began talking about missions and planning to go overseas. When God opened the door, I went. I have since visited nine countries, and our teaching material has now been distributed in over 50 nations.

We must all begin somewhere. It can be compared to the passage in Mark that describes the sower sowing the Word. When the Word is received, some bring forth 30-, some 60- and some 100-fold (Mark 4:14-20). We all begin at the lowest level and progress into the fulness of God's will, blessings and purpose. Your level of blessing will be determined by your desire to pursue spiritual truth.

Are you going to date or romance? Are you going to kiss or cleave?

GOING BUT NOT KNOWING

When God instructed Abraham to depart from Ur, Abraham obeyed, not knowing where he was going (Hebrews 11:8). When he got there, however, he knew he was in the right place. God would speak to Abraham and say, "This is the place; stay here for awhile." Then, as God led him, he would pull up stakes and the tent caravan would be on the move again. They stopped only when God commanded them to.

There are times when we, too, go out in faith with no idea what the future holds! When Naomi arrived at Bethlehem, she was a wounded woman. Ten years of famine, death and loneliness were etched in her face. The entire city must have been moved when they saw her (Ruth 1:19). Although no one knew her true story, gossip had fueled rumors for years. "Have you heard about Naomi? She backslid and went to Moab. Someone said she and her husband were having trouble."

Friends from her past began to interrogate her about her 10-year absence. Brokenly, she replied,

DON'T CALL ME NAOMI, BUT CALL ME MARA (RUTH 1:20).

Her reply reveals she had lost touch with her previous identity. Naomi's heart cried, "I went out [from Bethlehem] full, and the Lord has brought me home again empty" (Ruth 1:20). She was not the same woman her former neighbors knew. Life had been cruel to her.

Ten years before, most people remained to endure the famine, but Naomi and her family left. Likewise, people leave a church when things get rough. Seldom is it because the Lord really tells them to go. They leave because they are offended, hurt or perhaps because of internal strife. Frequently, after several years, they return . . . carrying wounds and hurts that have never totally healed. Having lost their former identity in the house of God, they return broken and in despair.

Bethlehem was Naomi's home, yet it did not feel like home. Bitterness and sorrow can blur your perception of what God has done and what He will do. Naomi left as the wife of Elimelech and returned as a widow. She owned a house and land when she departed, but returned empty-handed. She held her head up before the famine, but 10 years later, her head was hanging low under the weight of bitterness, bankruptcy and brokenness.

Then there was Ruth. This beautiful, dark-complected, dark-haired Moabite, listened patiently as Naomi spoke of her own woes. Hurting inside, Ruth had no one to talk to. Nobody was comforting her for her loss and for what she had gone through.

Ruth, however, did not look for pity. There is no reason to believe her motive for following Naomi was anything more than a genuine love and concern for her mother-in-law. She did not know that God had already planned for her to meet a handsome Bethlehemite to marry and start a royal family.

Naomi probably never realized that standing in her shadow was a young woman who, though a stranger from a cursed land, would become one of the greatest women in Israel's history. Ruth was the best thing to ever happen to Naomi and the best thing that had happened in Bethlehem up to that time.

Ruth and Naomi were two women linked by a common bond. The lives of these two emotionally-drained handmaidens had been woven together by the thread of sorrow; now they were together back in Bethlehem, the place where the sovereign hand of God would begin to fulfill a destiny that would change the world!

When you leave Moab . . . and your past . . . behind, when you cross the Jordan to journey to the place where God is leading you, you will discover the key to your future. To discover your purpose, you must be at the right place at the right time. Only by being sensitive to the leading of God's Spirit can you find yourself there.

Chapter 3

The Progression of the Blessing

Timing and personal connections play a large role in a person's destiny. This was especially true for Ruth and Naomi. In the midst of Naomi's mourning, however, she had forgotten about her affiliation with an important *kingdom connection*. This connection would prove to be the source of her miracle.

His name was Boaz. A near kinsman, he was a relative of her departed husband. Was the timing of Ruth and Naomi's arrival planned from their perspective, or was it coincidental? They arrived in Bethlehem *just as the barley fields were about to be harvested*. As it turned out, Boaz owned a large field.

Someone out there has a key to the door of your heart. Someone has a word of wisdom to bring peace to your mind. Someone has a revelation from the Lord that will give you confirmation as you strive to be led of the Lord. There is a Boaz in Bethlehem looking for you!

> AND NAOMI HAD A KINSMAN OF HER HUSBAND'S, A MIGHTY MAN OF WEALTH, OF THE FAMILY OF ELIMELECH; AND HIS NAME WAS BOAZ (RUTH 2:1).

Boaz was a wealthy businessman. He was also a relative. Apparently, Naomi had never told Ruth about Boaz, so it is safe to conclude that Ruth made the long journey from Moab to Bethlehem with pure motives. She was not thinking about meeting and marrying a wealthy Jew. She was staying with Naomi because they were family. This must have touched Boaz; it certainly touched the heart of God.

MOTIVES AND HIDDEN AGENDAS

In sharp contrast to Ruth's pure motives, are people who link up with someone for what that individual can do for them. Man's nature compels us to search out that person, business or ministry that is in the limelight.

It is easy to jump on a caravan when it is well publicized because we like to be up front. We like the attention we receive. We want the whole world to notice our talents. Be warned, however, if this is your motive for ministry then you have already received your reward (Matthew 6:2-5). Ruth had no hidden plan or secret agenda. She was there to be a blessing. Her heart of servitude fit perfectly with the plan of God.

When I met my wife, one thing greatly impressed me—her pure intentions. Being a young single minister had fringe benefits. One of those perks came in the form of abundant invitations to enjoy a home-cooked meal. I soon discovered, however, that some of these dinner invitations came with a catch. There were mothers who held to the old saying, "The quickest way to a man's heart is through his stomach."

I soon learned that their motive was to hook me up with their single daughter. These mothers would talk about how they wanted their daughters to meet a godly young man. I would eat, smile and leave, thinking, "Good meal but no deal!"

In those days, yearly camp meeting was a time and place for young people to meet. Sometimes young girls competed with each other to see who could go out with one of the many young ministers. This was disturbing, because some of the girls were only interested in being able to say, "I went out with so and so," not in the minister as a person.

Like Ruth, Pam had different, purer motives. When I told her I loved her, she shared it with only her two sisters and the lady she stayed with. People in her church had to question her about how I was doing and how I felt about her. She was very private and personal about our conversations and our relationship. Like Mary, Pam hid these things in her heart. Pam was not looking for a preacher, but she got one. One reason I was so attracted to her was because she was not chasing every young man who crossed her path. She had no desire to become a "preacher's wife." She had no selfish motive about our relationship.

She was in love with Perry Stone, the man; not just Perry Stone, the preacher.

To this day, she continues to minister behind the scenes with her gentle spirit. Some women (and men) tell everything they know. They want others to know that they know everything! The Bible calls them "silly women" who run from house to house telling everything they know about everybody they know (2 Timothy 3:6). That is not what God needs or a man wants in a woman.

God wants women who, like Ruth, have a gentle and quiet spirit, one that a person can confide in (1 Peter 3:4). Some people want information to use against a person, but the spirit of Ruth is one of kindness and gentleness.

Boaz was a special man who needed a special woman. Boaz was a strong leader. He did not need a strong female personality beside him to compete with. Boaz knew what he was doing. He needed a woman like Ruth, who was willing to work beside him as he pursued the will of God for himself and his family.

For the first three years of my ministry, I thought I had to marry a woman with abundant talent. I would carefully observe any single girl who could sing and play the keyboards. It took a few years for me to discover that I didn't necessarily need someone with great musical ability, but I did need a woman with a temperate disposition.

I needed someone who would support me when the message didn't go well, when the crowds were down and the altars were empty. When the offerings wouldn't pay the bills and the journey back home was long and difficult, talent alone would not see us through. In times such as these, a beautiful voice and a mastery of the keyboard would not matter! I realized I needed a woman who would hold my hand, snuggle next to me and say, "Its okay, baby. I'm with you and I know God has something better just around the corner."

I needed an encourager. Ruth's very presence made Naomi feel better. Ruth would not hurry, but had the patience to wait for God's will. The Bible reveals that Ruth knew how to respect and respond to a man. I concluded that this was what I needed in a wife.

THE THREE-FOLD BLESSING PROGRESSION

Naomi returned to her city in the time of the barley harvest (Ruth 1:22). She was in the right place at the right time. Bethlehem, the house of bread, was known for its fields of barley and wheat. The seven feasts of Israel revolve around the times of harvesting. The Feast of Passover falls during the barley harvest, while the Feast of Pentecost falls during the wheat harvest. If you're looking for bread, go to where grain is being harvested!

There in Bethlehem, Ruth discovered a progression in the blessing of God. Searching the Scriptures, it is clear that God's favor comes to those who are obedient in little things (Matthew 25:21-23). Once we learn to walk through the small doors, God will open up larger ones for us.

The movement and progression of our blessings are dependent on our last act of obedience. God will only give more after we have followed previous instructions.

Though she was from Moab, Ruth understood the principles of God. She knew that in order to obtain success, you must have two elements working on your behalf. Ruth asked for grace (Ruth 2:2) and for favor (2:13). Favor opens the door but grace keeps the door open! Ruth also knew that there were certain things that she was going to have to do.

In chapter 2 of Ruth, we detect the principle of 30-, 60- and 100-fold blessing. This principle is explained in the Gospel of Mark. Jesus revealed this when He preached about the sower who planted the seed, which is the Word (Mark 4:3-8).

Having stood in Galilee where this message was preached, I can visualize the effect it had on the people there. In this open-air setting, Christ spoke about a man planting seed. Today, there is a large farm at the base of the hill where Jesus preached, and wheat is grown there.

❏ JESUS SPOKE OF THE SEED FALLING ON STONES. THE GALILEE REGION IS COVERED WITH LARGE, BLACK BASALT STONES. THEY OFTEN REST IN THE CENTER OF THE FIELDS WHERE FARMERS ATTEMPT TO PLANT SEEDS.

❏ CHRIST MENTIONED BIRDS WHO WOULD SWOOP DOWN AND DEVOUR THE SEEDS BEFORE THEY COULD TAKE ROOT IN THE SOIL. DURING PLANTING SEASON, IT IS COMMON TO SEE, IN THE SAME AREA WHERE JESUS PREACHED, LARGE FLOCKS OF BIRDS HOVERING IN THE AIR, WATCHING THE FARMERS SOW THE SEED. IF THE SEED IS NOT PROTECTED, THE BIRDS WILL SWOOP DOWN AND STEAL IT.

❑ THE PARABLE OF THE SOWER MENTIONS THE HEAT OF THE SUN THAT BEATS DOWN ON THE GROUND, PARCHING THE SEED, AND CAUSING IT TO DIE BEFORE IT PRODUCES FRUIT. THE GALILEE DISTRICT CAN EXPERIENCE HOT, DRY SEASONS, AND EVEN DROUGHT.

As Jesus preached the parable of the sower, He painted a beautiful illustration for His listeners. Everything He spoke about could be seen before the eyes of the people. Jesus then revealed that if the seed of the Word took root, it would always produce. In fact, it would produce "some thirtyfold, some sixty, and some a hundred" (Mark 4:8).

The level of blessing is not measured solely by the amount of seed planted, but it is also determined by the condition of the soil, or the heart of the person receiving the Word. The story of Ruth reveals the three-fold level of increase upon those who are willing to hear, plant and obey the Word of God.

The Principle of Increase

For the earth yields crops by itself: first the blade, then the head, after that the full grain in the head. But when the grain ripens, immediately he puts in the sickle, because the harvest has come (MARK 4:28, 29).

This passage of scripture explains the principle of increase from 30-fold to 100-fold. It shows that once the seed is planted in the ground and the weather conditions are correct, the seed begins a threefold process:

❏ First, the blade

❏ Then , the head, the ear or stalk

❏ Then, the full grain, the corn or mature fruit

The blade represents the 30-fold level; the stalk represents the 60-fold level and the mature fruit represents the 100-fold level. Once the seed reaches maturity and becomes a ripe ear, then it can be picked from the stalk and eaten. Or, the ear can be used as seed for the future harvest. One ear of corn can produce dozens of plants that can, in turn, produce hundreds of ears.

People can eat their seed or they can replenish it by a continual planting process. People who never tithe or give are always eating their seed. They never plant any seed into their future. Since the story of Ruth shows the miracle of increase, the three stages of growing can be observed in Ruth's life. Applying this pattern to Ruth, we see her beginning in the corner of the field as the blade. Her "handfuls of purpose" was the stalk. But when Boaz "laid it on her", she had matured into the fruit (Ruth 3:15).

MOVING FROM THE SEED TO THE MATURE FRUIT

Your life in Christ should progress forward and increase continually. It should not be put on hold while you wait for an open door. After traveling for over 28 years in full-time ministry, I have conversed with hundreds of young people who felt a call into the ministry. I have shared my personal testimony with them and encouraged them to pursue the inner burden they felt.

Sometimes, I would return to the church years later, only to find that they were still waiting for the Lord to "open the door." When I remind them that the local jail, nursing home or their own church's bus ministry provides an opportunity for them to minister, most reply, "That's not my call. I am called to preach like you do, behind a pulpit."

This makes me realize they were not actually called to preach. Preaching behind the pulpit is the most common type of ministry, but Jesus said, "Go into all the world" (Mark 16:15). Almost 90 percent of all preachers worldwide live in America. Why don't some of those who want to preach, go out where the harvest is? They have a zeal for God, but not a direct call of God. To move into the full blessing of God requires complete obedience!

In the late 1980s, I conducted a yearly revival at the Upper Room Church in Orange County, California. There I met a young man named Jonathan Augustine. Jonathan attended the revival every night faithfully. In the course of the meeting,

I discovered that he would go to a large youth hangout and preach on the street to the young people. Often he was mocked, laughed at and criticized, but he would not hold back because the Word of God burned in him like a fire.

I told his pastor, the Reverend Floyd Lawhon, that God was going to use this young man because he was faithful in the little things. During a special service, the bishop of a large denomination in Bulgaria spoke at this same church. He invited anyone who would to come and minister in Bulgaria.

Jonathan felt the burden and the urge to answer the call. He packed up and set off for Bulgaria, and ended up staying for several months. Miraculously, the Lord began to give him the ability to speak the Bulgarian language. He took a small church and built it up to about 500 people.

Jonathan returned to America to further his education, and while here, he met a lovely Bulgarian girl. They were married, and today they have a handsome son. He and his wife are now overseeing a Bible school and are making a powerful impact on people's lives in this eastern European nation! What Jonathan has accomplished began with a dream — a tiny seed planted in fertile soil. As he obeyed the Lord, that seed began to sprout until now, a great harvest has been realized.

The trouble with some is that they want to eat the fruit before they plant the seed. They wish to walk into a wheat-laden field and reap, yet they will not take the time to plow up the stones, stumps and hindrances that will prevent their seed from growing.

THE LAW OF GLEANING

There are those lean times when situations beyond our control dictate to us what we must do. During these times, there may not be a field to plow. We may have no seed to plant. But even in these situations, God has provided a spiritual principle that will allow us, if we are obedient, to get back on our feet.

God established a law through Moses called the law of gleaning. When a man harvested his field he was to allow the four corners to remain unharvested so that the poor, the widows and the strangers could glean in the field (Leviticus 19:9, 10). As a poor stranger, Ruth went out, according to the law and custom, to glean in the field. Notice the divine "set-up" in the location of her gleaning.

> SO SHE DEPARTED AND WENT AND GLEANED IN THE FIELD AFTER THE REAPERS; AND SHE HAPPENED TO COME TO THE PORTION OF THE FIELD BELONGING TO BOAZ, WHO WAS OF THE FAMILY OF ELIMELECH (RUTH 2:3, NASB).

FOCUSED ON YOUR ASSIGNMENT

During her first days in Bethlehem, Ruth was hired to glean in the fields. Given this opportunity, Ruth became so focused on her assignment that she didn't have time for a lot of social activity. Usually after work, the reapers and the young ladies would gather together for fellowship, but notice what Boaz told Ruth:

> LET YOUR EYES BE ON THE FIELD WHICH THEY REAP, AND GO AFTER THEM. HAVE I NOT COMMANDED THE YOUNG MEN NOT

TO TOUCH YOU? AND WHEN YOU ARE THIRSTY, GO TO THE VESSELS AND DRINK FROM WHAT THE YOUNG MEN HAVE DRAWN (RUTH 2:9).

Due to hard work, her beauty, or both, she immediately got the attention of Boaz. She gleaned from "morning till evening" (Ruth 2:7). When she had an opportunity to take a break, she spent "a little" time "in the house" (Ruth 2:7). While he was attracted to her appearance, Boaz didn't overlook her work ethic.

I was called into the ministry at age 16. From that moment, I became disconnected with all public school activities. I had little or no social life. I stayed in an office or my bedroom, studying for hours on end. At the time, I was not evangelizing, traveling or preaching. During this time, I was learning to defeat "bears and lions" in personal, private battles.

It would be some time before there was a Goliath to kill that would launch my ministry into the public eye (see 1 Samuel 16). Yet, Jesus was watching my every move. He saw my desire to accomplish great things for the Kingdom. In fact, I was so focused on the harvest fields where I ministered, I didn't date during my revivals. I did not want to be distracted from my mission. Those years of almost complete isolation have ceased. I now have a beautiful wife, a son and daughter. God has blessed this ministry to reach thousands of people around the world. I believe it is because of my total commitment to the assignment I have been given.

Leaders of great ministries and pastors of large churches have told me it is difficult to find a secretary, an office manager or workers who will stay committed to the task at hand. It is just as difficult to find people who will work hard and help carry the burden of the ministry. Sad to say, some people take little pride in their accomplishments for God. It seems they simply work for a paycheck and that's all.

Others are "biding their time" where they are, waiting until God opens a bigger and better door for them. When that opportunity comes, there they go. We have many friends who own both small and large businesses, as well as those who direct large ministries. A common challenge they share is not being able to find good workers to help with the demands of the business or the ministry. Businessmen, such as Boaz, are always looking for workers who will WORK. Ruth was a dedicated worker. Remember, except for the grain she collected, she wasn't getting paid for her labor! In fact, the portion of grain she collected was taken home to Naomi. She was doing the work for someone else's benefit!

When will we learn that God rewards those who work faithfully and with pure motives (Hebrews 11:5)? It has been reported that only five percent of the working people in America are completely happy in their field of labor. It doesn't take a genius to figure out that 95 percent are working strictly out of necessity. Their only goal is to get a paycheck to pay bills, and to provide for the family. Yet, it doesn't have to be this way.

If we follow the leading of God's Spirit, we could all be laboring in a field that is challenging, but fulfilling. Some may be in the right place and just don't realize it, due to a lack of concentration. When you concentrate on your assignment, it becomes a part of you. Then you will find contentment. Not only that, those who are over you, your employer and God, take notice.

ADVANCE IN YOUR FIELD OF LABOR

I once said to a person we were hiring in our office, "I pay people according to the problems they solve and not the problems they create." If you desire to move up in your job and increase, then let your supervisor see that you have a desire to help the company INCREASE. These seven nuggets may help.

- ❏ LEARN EVERYTHING YOU CAN ABOUT THE JOB ASSIGNED TO YOU. LEARN MORE THAN YOU NEED TO KNOW AND LEARN MORE THAN YOU ARE EXPECTED TO KNOW. MOST BUSINESSES AND MINISTRIES ADVANCE PEOPLE IN PAY WHEN THEY SEE THE PERSON QUALIFYING THEMSELVES BY INCREASING THEIR KNOWLEDGE OF THE AREA OF WORK IN WHICH THEY ARE INVOLVED.

- ❏ OFFER TO DO ABOVE AND BEYOND WHAT YOU ARE EXPECTED TO DO. WHATEVER YOUR HANDS FIND TO DO, THEN DO IT.

- ❏ TRY TO SOLVE PROBLEMS THAT MAKE IT EASIER ON THOSE OVER YOU. SOLVE PROBLEMS INSTEAD OF CREATING THEM.

- ❑ DISCOVER WHEN AND WHERE THE NEXT PROMOTION IS COMING FROM, AND POSITION YOURSELF WITH THE WISDOM AND KNOWLEDGE NEEDED TO EXPERIENCE THAT INCREASE.

- ❑ DETERMINE THAT IF YOU ARE "CALLED" TO A PLACE OR A MINISTRY, YOU WILL STAY WITH THAT CHURCH, MINISTRY OR BUSINESS, EVEN IN THE TOUGHEST OF TIMES. IF YOU RUN AWAY DURING TOUGH TIMES, YOU WILL RUN FROM PROBLEMS FOR THE REST OF YOUR LIFE. BY LEAVING TOO SOON, YOU COULD BE LEAVING YOUR FIELD OF BLESSING.

- ❑ FACE ANY MISUNDERSTANDING IN LOVE, BEFORE IT GETS OUT OF HAND. SOME PEOPLE ALWAYS CONFRONT. OUR MINISTRY IS NOT ONE OF CONFRONTATION, BUT OF RECONCILIATION. WE ARE NOT CALLED TO STRAIGHTEN THINGS OUT, BUT TO HEAL AND TO RECONCILE SITUATIONS. ASK QUESTIONS AND MAKE STATEMENTS IN LOVE, NOT IN SPITE.

- ❑ NEVER SPEAK OF ANOTHER WORKER OF STAFF MEMBER BEHIND HIS OR HER BACK. NEVER SAY ANYTHING ABOUT SOME ONE THAT YOU WOULD BE EMBARRASSED BY IF THEY KNEW YOU SAID IT. ALWAYS REMEMBER, PEOPLE TALK. WHEN YOU TELL SOMEONE, "THIS IS BETWEEN YOU AND ME," YOU SHOULD CONSIDER THAT HUMAN NATURE FINDS IT DIFFICULT TO REMAIN SILENT BECAUSE INFORMATION IS POWER. BE CAREFUL WHAT YOU SAY AND TO WHOM YOU SAY IT. REMEMBER, YOU NEVER HAVE TO APOLOGIZE FOR WHAT YOU NEVER SAID.

Finally, love the work where God has placed you. Enjoy whatever it is you do. If you dread going to work, you should pray for a change and discover what you are happy doing.

Chapter 4

Two Keys Bring Seven Blessings

Before Ruth experienced a great breakthrough with Boaz, she asked for both GRACE and FAVOR.

LET ME GO TO THE FIELD, AND GLEAN HEADS OF GRAIN AFTER HIM IN WHOSE SIGHT I MAY FIND FAVOR.

THEN SHE SAID [TO BOAZ], "LET ME FIND FAVOR IN YOUR SIGHT. . . ."

BLESSED BE THE ONE WHO TOOK NOTICE OF YOU. . . (RUTH 2:2, 10, 13, 19).

Grace is the unmerited divine blessing that comes from God to you. Favor is the unearned blessings given to you by men. The Bible says men shall "give into your bosom" (Luke 6:38). The source of all blessings is the Lord, yet the flow comes through the hands of men. Thus, we can see it is possible for us to live with the favor of both God and man.

Favor Can Stop Death

❏ Daniel interpreted a king's dream and saved the wise men in Babylon (Daniel 2:24).

❏ Queen Esther delivered the Hebrews in Persia because she confronted the king, made intercession for her people and exposed a Satanic plot against them (Esther 5:2).

❏ The church interceded for Peter, and God spared his life from death, delivering him about 12 hours before he was scheduled to be beheaded (Acts 12:1-18).

Favor Can Bring Great Financial Blessing

In 24 hours, Ruth went from being a single stranger to being the most famous woman in the city. Favor with Boaz brought blessing into her private life. When Jacob worked with Laban in Syria, the financial increase began to pour into Laban's entire household and all his property. Laban admitted that the reason for this blessing was because Jacob, a Hebrew, was working for him.

Laban said, "For I have learned by experience that the Lord has blessed me for your sake" (Genesis 30:27). Jacob replied, "For what you had before I came was little, and it has increased to a great amount; the LORD has blessed you since my coming" (Genesis 30:30).

Perhaps the company you work for has experienced increases because YOU have been connected with them. God may be blessing businesses because He has tithers and givers sitting in the offices and directing the matters of the company. Therefore God keeps the company financially strong so His people can give and tithe for the Kingdom's work.

FAVOR CAN BRING A DOUBLE BLESSING

Job's blessing was lost by a battle but regained by Divine favor. In fact, the increase after the battle was "twice as much as he had before" (Job 42:10). Elisha received a double portion of the anointing of Elijah (2 Kings 2). Elisha found favor because he stayed with the prophet until the very end. While many sons of the prophets viewed Elijah from afar, Elisha followed Elijah until the end and the double portion blessing fell on him.

FAVOR CAN SPEED UP YOUR DESTINY

You may have waited for years to see the promises of God come to pass in your life. One act of God's supernatural favor, however, can move you from obscurity to prominence. Esther saved the Hebrews because she stood before the king. Ruth married a wealthy businessman and became famous in Bethlehem because of one night of favor.

Joseph went from the pit, to a prison, to the palace . . . because he found great favor. God revealed Joseph's future in a dream but the dream got him in trouble with his family. He ended up in an Egyptian prison. Yet, God used Joseph's ability to interpret dreams to reach Pharaoh. The gift that seemed to bring such trouble was instrumental, 17 years later, in making Joseph second-in-command over all of Egypt.

In his early beginnings, Billy Graham preached a tent revival in Los Angeles, California. Media magnate William Randolph Hearst sent a memo to his newspapers, telling his writers to "puff Graham." The *Los Angeles Times* published an article favorable to Graham's revival, and the story hit the national news wires. Overnight, Billy Graham was recognized as a powerful evangelist.

Sometimes, what looks bad is turned around for our good when the favor of God is upon us. Oral Roberts embarked on his evangelistic fame in 1948 during a tent revival in Oklahoma. One night, a man fired a shot from a gun at Roberts, missing him by inches.

The local newspaper report of the incident eventually spread across the nation. Within 24 hours, the nation knew of a young man who prayed for the sick and got results. The revival went for nine weeks, and the name *Oral Roberts* became known from coast to coast. The favor of God can turn a curse into a blessing!

Favor Can Cause the Impossible to Happen

God can show up and bring favor in a situation that seems impossible. Once I was in Africa when I had to return home unexpectedly because of the illness of a loved one. The only flight out was over-booked. Upon learning this, the bishop of the nation went with me to the airlines office. He knew that the people in the office had heard me preach on television.

The bishop told them, "If you want this man back to minister in our nation, then you will get him a seat right now." Five hours later, I was escorted through a large crowd to the front of a line and put on the best seat in the economy section. Had we met the wrong person at the wrong time, I would have been stuck there for three more days. God set us up with the right person at the right time and gave us favor.

Favor Comes Through Prayer

Being born again does not necessarily guarantee favor. Favor is like wisdom: you are not born with it, but it can be given to you by the Lord if you ask Him for it.

Before traveling to a church, I ask God to give me favor with the people. The message I am preaching will be a blessing only if the people receive what I am saying. If they don't like me they won't hear what I am saying.

Before a major decision, ask God for favor. Before speaking, ask God for favor. Before a business meeting, ask God for favor. God may move someone out of your way before the meeting and place the right person in your path, because of favor.

We once had a person working with us who prayed constantly for favor. When the Post Office or the printers would mess things up, she would go directly to them and get more done in one trip than we could with five phone calls. I would ask her, "How did you get that done?" She replied, "I have the favor of God."

Favor Doesn't Exempt You from Trouble

Some people feel that if they are in God's will, they are exempt from problems. Others believe that if they have the favor of God, everything will always go right. This is not true. Sometimes, even with favor, we will experience troubles. The reason I know I am blessed is not because I am exempt from trouble, but because I keep making it through the storms. My boat has been cracked and filled with water, but I have made it to the other side.

Occasionally, I get beat up by people, but I keep running the race. I am blessed; I have survived terrible attacks and still walk with victory. Having favor is not a ticket of exemption from physical or spiritual attacks. It is the assurance that God, who is with you, will see you through in spite of these attacks! Are you ready to trust God and move forward to where you need to be?

Chapter 5

Getting Out
of the Corner

Some people have a spirit that says, *I have my own plans and agendas. I have my own ministry.* It's me . . . me . . . me! Their self-centered lifestyles soon become evident as they begin to pull away from their God-appointed job or ministry in order to pursue their own self-appointed plans.

In contrast, some labor faithfully in the assignment God has given them. Perhaps you are one of these. Most of the time, it seems your labor goes unnoticed and your efforts unrewarded. Your level of blessing may be at 30-fold. You may be in an isolated corner of the harvest field where it seems no one is paying attention. Yet, you are working and striving because you have an assignment from God, not because you are seeking attention.

You are ministering to Naomi. Someone hurting needs you near them. Your vision and future are inconsequential; your heart is concerned with changing the heart of another. Boaz (Jesus) is starting you off at the 30-fold level. He sees you in the corner. He is protecting you from the wrong men and women. He is providing for you because you are in HIS field!

The 30-fold level is the gleaning level. Keep the faith, for you will not always be in the corner alone, working for someone else. God has you marked for increase. When Boaz began to recognize Ruth's presence, she asked a question.

WHY HAVE I FOUND FAVOR IN YOUR EYES, THAT YOU SHOULD TAKE NOTICE OF ME, SINCE I AM A FOREIGNER (RUTH 2:10)?

Boaz' answer reveals how the Lord looks on those who minister to others in need. Ruth had three marks against her. She was a woman, she was a Moabite and she was a widow. She lost her financial security when she lost her husband, she lost her identity when she left Moab, and being a woman made her vulnerable.

Most women in her situation would be out hunting a husband who could bring security and meet her needs. Not Ruth! She was different, and that was the very reason Boaz took notice of her.

AND BOAZ ANSWERED AND SAID TO HER, "IT HAS BEEN FULLY REPORTED TO ME, ALL THAT YOU HAVE DONE FOR YOUR MOTHER-IN-LAW SINCE THE DEATH OF YOUR HUSBAND, AND HOW YOU HAVE LEFT YOUR FATHER AND YOUR MOTHER AND THE LAND OF YOUR BIRTH, AND HAVE COME TO A PEOPLE WHOM YOU DID NOT KNOW BEFORE" (RUTH 2:11).

Boaz revealed what impressed him. Ruth was willing to separate herself from all she was familiar with, including friends and family, in order to minister to a hurting woman. Through Boaz, God was showing Ruth that her commitment was paying off. Through an unexpected source, Ruth was being ministered to. Seeing her dedication, Boaz spoke a prophetic blessing over her:

> THE LORD REPAY YOUR WORK, AND A FULL REWARD BE GIVEN YOU BY THE LORD GOD OF ISRAEL, UNDER WHOSE WINGS YOU HAVE COME FOR REFUGE (RUTH 2:12).

FAVOR MOVES YOU FORWARD

Ruth then asked Boaz, "Let me find favor in your sight" (Ruth 2:13). Favor is special approval. In response, Boaz invited Ruth into the house where she sat at the table with all the reapers and ate the food prepared from Boaz's table. The Bible says, "And she ate and was satisfied" (Ruth 2:14).

By gleaning in the corner of the field alone, she was experiencing a 30-fold level of blessing. This is the level of "JUST ENOUGH." This level is just enough to meet basic needs, just enough to get by, just enough for your "daily bread." Most believers live at this level.

The Israelites in Egypt lived at the level of "never enough." They were overworked and underpaid. They did not have straw to put in the mud bricks. The Egyptians hoarded all the wealth and food, and the Hebrews were their servants.

Ruth was a servant working in the corner of the harvest field, but she had the attention of Boaz. She gleaned just enough to meet her need, but God had something more for her. She had the attention of Boaz, who was ready to give her a promotion.

Be encouraged to know that someone near you has the ability to give you a promotion. Take strength in the fact that there is someone who will move you from the level where you are to a level of increase. Everyone starts in a gleaning corner, but with Boaz on your side, you are going to come out of the corner of 30-fold and go into a higher level of blessing.

The Sixty-Fold Level

The next day Ruth arose to perform her daily routine. On this day, however, a special, unexpected blessing awaited her.

> And when she rose up to glean, Boaz commanded his young men, saying, "Let her glean even among the sheaves, and do not reproach her. Also let grain from the bundles fall purposely for her; leave it that she may glean, and do not rebuke her" (Ruth 2:15, 16).

Boaz was breaking tradition. Strangers were allowed to glean only in a small corner after the main harvest was completed. Every stranger and widow in Bethlehem was permitted by the Law of Moses to glean a corner. But Boaz got Ruth out of the corner, and said, "Do not reproach her . . . do not rebuke her."

Had the reapers seen Ruth among the sheaves, they would have said, "What are you doing here? This is off limits to you, a stranger and a Moabite." They would have reminded her that her past and her that her place of birth hindered her progress. But Boaz instructed the men to leave her alone. Don't rebuke her, he said, don't bring up the fact she is a stranger among us. Make her comfortable. Let "handfuls on purpose" fall where she is gleaning!

Satan is the accuser of the brethren (Revelation 12:10). When he reminds us of our past, it hinders our progress into the future. Often, condemning feelings of guilt cloud our vision.

 People say, "If I had only done this, or if I hadn't done that." God is in the NOW! Hebrews 11:1 says: "NOW faith is." He cannot determine your future, so Satan tries to make you a prisoner of your past. When we live in the graveyard of the past, Satan torments us!

Boaz wanted to be sure Ruth's past was not brought up as she moved forward into the blessings prepared for her! He marked the spot where she was to work. When she was looking away, reapers would throw sheaves of grain on the ground near her feet—a sign of favor. The "boss" was recognizing her hard work and the commitment she had made. Without asking, she got additional grain anyway.

BLESSED ON PURPOSE

Boaz was blessing her on purpose! He was telling her, "You are a special person and I want to show you my appreciation for your spirit and your attitude."

I direct a major ministry. We have full-time workers who assist us in ministry. Some work in research, some in television-video outreach, others answer the mail, lay out the magazine, take phone orders, assist in the prayer ministry, singing, etc. For the past 20 years, we have had numerous people connected to our ministry, both in the office and on the road.

Occasionally, I have hired good people who treated the ministry like any other nine-to-five job. To them, it was their means of paying bills. Their attitude was, "Get me out by five. I'm tired of this place." When I see an attitude such as this, it weakens my resolve to want to bless that person with additional blessings. It reveals where their heart is or should I say, where it is not. I have told past workers, "When your love for our ministry is gone and you have no burden for the people, for their needs and for the work we are doing, it is time for you to move on."

On the other hand, when I see workers staying after normal business hours without being asked, and when I see those same people searching to find something they can do, both Pam and I have a desire to bless them beyond what the ministry is doing.

After 20 years of full-time ministry, Pam and I have observed two types of people. Those who come to be a blessing and those who want a blessing. Some attach themselves to the work for what the ministry can do for them. Others have a heart for the work of God, and desire to *be* a blessing. Local churches and ministries need people who are called into that ministry. Pastors do not need an associate pastor on staff who wants to start a church three blocks away after he has been linked with members of the congregation for three years! Pastors need men who say, "I am with you. I am called alongside you. We are a team. Your battles are my battles and your victories are my victories." When a pastor finds co-workers with that attitude, he should do all in his strength to minister to every need that arises in their lives.

Evangelistic ministries need people who are called to that ministry. Those organizations need people who will say, "If I never preach at your camp meeting, I am called. If I never sing before thousands, I am called. If you never brag on my ability, I am with you all the way!"

Ruth was called! She was chosen! She was a woman of destiny and she wasn't lazy. God doesn't choose lazy people to minister. He never calls a "couch potato." Moses was a busy shepherd, as was David. Levi was a busy tax collector while Peter was a fisherman who spent entire nights on the sea. God not only recognized the gift in each person but he recognized their inner character and their willingness to work.

All who have a worldwide ministry are almost obsessed with their desire to reach the lost. Paul talked about being "addicted to the gospel" (1 Corinthians 16:15). God calls men who will WORK in the field. Jesus is asking, "Why have you been standing here idle all day" (Matthew 20:6)? Younger ministers visit our ministry center and see the level we are on now. What they can't see is the prayer, fasting and effort of non-stop ministry that has brought us to this point. It is difficult for them to see past our new ministry center to the bedroom in my father's old house where it all started 28 years ago. There is a price to pay to get to the next level.

Ruth went into the field every day. As the midday sun beamed rays of unbearable heat on her face, she labored. It was Boaz who invited her into the house for rest. She didn't ask for anything, she just did her job. She arose early and stayed out until the sunset. Boaz, and God, recognized her hard work.

Men of vision promote those of like vision. Boaz's life centered around his vision of the harvest. His yearly income was wrapped up in a large field of grain. To touch the heart of Boaz, you had to show him how faithful you were in the field! The Lord is looking for people who will love souls and minister to the poor. The Bible says whoever ministers to the poor "lends to the Lord" (Proverbs 19:17). The Lord will reward those who seek the harvest first!

> Seek first the kingdom of God and His righteousness, and all these things shall be added to you (Matthew 6:33).

Ruth moved to the next level of increase. It was the 60-fold level, between 30-fold and 100-fold. It is better than 30, but not quite as good as 100-fold. It is INCREASE, nonetheless. Tangible blessings were beginning to flow. She was working at the same pace, yet she was receiving additional handfuls on purpose.

Scripture says she gleaned an "ephah of barley" (Ruth 2:17). An *ephah* was approximately five gallons, much more than she had before. When she went into the city to show Naomi, the Bible says, "So she brought out and gave to her what she had kept back after she had been satisfied" (Ruth 2:18). Prior to this, she had just enough. Now, she had "enough and then some!" God is a God of increase. As my friend, Jentezen Franklin, has said, "God is all sufficient. He is El Shaddai and not El Cheapo."

THE WILL OF GOD—INCREASE

The Lord is a God of INCREASE. Before attacking Job, Satan recognized the blessings of the Lord on everything Job touched. Satan said, "His possessions have increased in the land" (Job 1:10). The Enemy recognizes progress and increase. The devil knows that your increase means you will have a realm of influence. Your influence can affect the decisions of others.

People listen to those who have influence. Successful people listen to those with a testimony of HOW success came to them. They know that results come only through tests and trials! The Biblical principle is that great testing comes before great blessing.

MOSES SPENT 40 YEARS IN A WILDERNESS, ALONE, BEFORE HE WAS RAISED UP TO PASTOR THREE MILLION PEOPLE (EXODUS 2, 3).

DAVID HIT ZIKLAG, WHERE HE LOST ALL HE HAD, BEFORE HE TOOK THE THRONE ON MOUNT ZION (1 SAMUEL 30:1-4).

RUTH LOST HER HUSBAND, BEFORE SHE MET HER BOAZ.

But God is a God of increase! He will never leave you with less. It may seem that you are on a decline, that you have less than ever before. But can you be determined like Ruth? Can you work alone in the gleaning corner? Can you minister to another's needs and ignore your own? Can you enjoy isolation from friends and family, knowing that God will eventually increase you?

Many scriptures speak about increase (see Psalm 115:14, Proverbs 18:20, 1 Corinthians 3:6 and 1 Thessalonians 3:12). The widow in 2 Kings 4 was about to lose her home and two sons to her creditors. But a prophet of God had a plan and God had the provision. A supernatural oil supply broke forth in her home. She was able to sell the oil to pay her bills. That is "enough!" But then she is told to "live on the rest" (2 Kings 4:7). That is increase!

The 60-fold level is the ability to meet your needs and have something left over! God has promised to "supply our need," but don't be satisfied with merely having your needs met. Get excited about the possibility of having enough and then some!

MOVING TO THE HIGHEST LEVEL OF BLESSING

The highest level of blessing is the 100-fold level. This represents the level of total provision, as well as the level where you become a blessing to others. It is the realm of increase to where your "cup is running over" (Psalms 23:5). It is where you are blessed in order to be a blessing.

When Boaz is with you, you will eventually move to the highest level of increase, the 100-fold level! When Ruth showed Naomi how she was blessed, Naomi asked who was helping her and bringing about this increase. Ruth informed Naomi that her benefactor was Boaz. Naomi was thrilled because Boaz was her near kinsman—a relative of Naomi's deceased husband.

It was a divine set-up. It was a pre-arranged, God moment. Ruth was unaware of God's purpose for her. She did not move to Bethlehem with a pre-conceived idea, saying, "I can get a rich Jew to marry me and provide for me." In fact, most Jews of that day would never have considered marrying a foreign woman. It would have been a disgrace for them to marry outside their own race.

God's law was so strict that even the High Priest was not permitted to marry a Jewish woman who had divorced or who was widowed, unless her previous husband had been a priest. Ruth must have known the odds were against her, but God had a plan. Ruth was willing to believe in the God of Naomi, and God was willing to use this woman because she acted in faith.

"Though your beginning was small, yet your latter end would increase abundantly" (Job 8:7). When God blesses you, He has your future in mind. We live a day at a time, but God is visionary. We pray, "Give us our daily bread," and cannot peer into the future to determine where we are going. But God's blessings are for our future. He who "declares the end from the beginning and the beginning from the end," has already seen the future.

A Spark Of New Hope

When Naomi heard that Boaz had noticed Ruth, a new hope sprang forth in her heart. When Naomi's husband died, she lost the family property in Bethlehem. The land remained in the name of the husband and was passed on as an inheritance to the oldest son. Because of her son's death, however, there was no one to claim the inheritance. God had established a law of redemption. If a woman lost her husband and had no children, she was to marry a brother of the deceased so she could have sons to carry on her husband's name. If there was no brother to marry, she could redeem her property back through the process of the kinsman-redeemer. A kinsman-redeemer was a next-of-kin who could, through a legal rite at the gate of the city, redeem the lost inheritance back to its original owner. In this case, the original owner was Naomi. Boaz was the kinsman-redeemer. As Ruth continued to labor in the field, God's perfect plan began to come into focus.

> [BOAZ] ALSO SAID TO ME, "YOU SHALL STAY CLOSE BY MY YOUNG MEN UNTIL THEY HAVE FINISHED ALL MY HARVEST" (RUTH 2:21).

Don't leave your divine appointment too early. When you are talented and dedicated to God, you will gain the attention of people in other fields. From other churches you will hear, "We need you here." They will try to impart their vision into you and say, "You can be more effective with us. We are a larger ministry and a larger church. Think of the results you can have in our field!" You must stay in the area God has placed you until the end of the mission. An early departure may result in an aborted destiny.

NAOMI SAID TO RUTH . . . , "IT IS GOOD, MY DAUGHTER, THAT YOU GO OUT WITH HIS YOUNG WOMEN, AND THAT PEOPLE DO NOT MEET YOU IN ANY OTHER FIELD."

All fields are not the same. All churches are not the same. All ministries are not the same. Ruth could have jumped from field to field, but she remained true to one person, Boaz. People often move prematurely. I tell pastors, "Never leave your church when you are discouraged . . . leave when everything is great." Men leave thinking the grass is greener on the other side, only to discover that sheep leave manure in every field!

People get frustrated and disgusted and begin to retaliate against those they are close to, and say, "I'll show them. I'll change churches. I'll show them, I'll go somewhere else." They leave before the appointed time and wind up miserable, missing the many blessings God had reserved for them.

Years ago, my father pastored a wonderful church in Virginia. Two members gave him problems, but the rest of the congregation were jewels. Dad allowed those two men to discourage him until he reached the point of deciding to move. He ended up going to five different churches over a period of about 12 years. These were good churches and good people, but he was never again fulfilled in pastoring.

He often said, "I should have waited on the Lord. I should not have been so hasty." Never make a decision to change the fields of labor just because another offer seems better, or because you are tired of where you are. Your blessing can only continue when you are where the Holy Spirit wants you.

FOLLOWING INSTRUCTIONS

Ruth received instructions well. She knew how to listen to those who had experience in their realms of expertise. She continued to work in the fields of Boaz.

SO SHE STAYED CLOSE BY THE YOUNG WOMEN OF BOAZ, TO GLEAN UNTIL THE END OF BARLEY HARVEST AND WHEAT HARVEST; AND SHE DWELT WITH HER MOTHER-IN-LAW (RUTH 2:23).

Don't jump from assignment to assignment. Don't go from church to church, attempting to find the perfect pastor. Don't run from ministry to ministry, looking for your blessing. Where has God planted you? Where does the anointing flow the best? More money or a better position is not always God's will. It is imperative to be in the right place at the right time! Seeing the potential for increase, Ruth refused to move to another field where she would have had to return to gleaning in a corner. In Boaz's field, she was seeing progression and favor favor from the head man. She was moving toward her destiny and must have sensed that something good was in the works.

Still, she knew it would require time. She knew she had to wait in order to see total fulfillment. Do you have the fortitude to wait on the Lord? If you feel called to preach, don't quit your job, leave home and believe God will open some mysterious door! God will open the right door when the time is right. Do what you are supposed to do until the appointed time.

Christ has the key of David and can open and close any door He desires (Revelation 3:8). Ruth was about to walk through the greatest door of her life!

Chapter 6

A Threshing Before the Final Blessing

Naomi knew the time had come for a breakthrough for herself and for Ruth. Boaz was the kingdom connection who could make it happen. A great restoration of what had been lost was coming. Naomi now had faith. A spark of hope was restored and Naomi's creativity began to flow. She began to plot a strategy for Ruth and Boaz to come together. Boaz could redeem the lost property for Naomi and Ruth was the key to open the door to Boaz's heart!

The critical time came at the end of the harvest as the reapers were winnowing. This is a process where the wheat and the chaff are separated. The process is performed at night when the wind picks up. The harvested sheaves are thrown into the wind. As the breeze hits the sheaves, the chaff is blown away as the coveted grain falls to the threshing floor.

The troubles and trials we experience in life eventually bring us to the threshing floor. This is where the good and bad, the wheat and the chaff, are separated. In each of us there exists positive and negative personality traits. We learn them in life, through circumstances and encounters with people.

Naomi was bitter due to her problems. That bitterness had to be sifted from her life. Likewise, you and I must be sifted so that the chaff in our lives can be removed. It is at that point that God can truly bless our lives like never before.

A BREAKDOWN COMES BEFORE A BREAKTHROUGH

Mark this down. Prior to your major *breakthrough,* there will be a major *breaking down* of your will.

This breaking down is used by God to mold your character. Somewhere in this process, there will be a long night when the wind is contrary to you. When the disciples were progressing to the "other side of the sea," the Bible says the "winds were contrary."

The storm hit in the darkest hour of the night. The Devil was trying to prevent the disciples from *going over*; and instead, he was trying to take them under. Yet, God used the wind to display His power. Even the stormy winds obey His voice.

The separation of the wheat from the chaff occurs at night when the wind blows and the darkness has settled around you. You cannot discern what is happening at the time, but those small storms and long nights alone are removing the impurities from you, so the fruit of the Spirit can come forth (Galatians 5:22-23). Boaz (Jesus) must separate the good from the bad, the wheat from the chaff in order to bring you to the 100-fold blessing!

We must take a trip to the threshing floor in order to become everything God intends. The chaff could be pride, rebellion or stubbornness. It could represent something that, if it surfaced down the road, could ruin your family, your life or your ministry. When John the Baptizer described Christ's ministry, he said:

> HIS WINNOWING FAN IS IN HIS HAND, AND HE WILL THOROUGHLY CLEAN OUT HIS THRESHING FLOOR, AND GATHER HIS WHEAT INTO THE BARN; BUT HE WILL BURN UP THE CHAFF WITH UNQUENCHABLE FIRE (MATTHEW 3:12).

What weakness do you have that raises its head from time to time? Do you have a short fuse in dealing with people? Are you quick to judge things prematurely? Do you, like Tarzan jumping from tree to tree, jump from mood swing to mood swing because of things you like and don't like? Before God uses you on a large scale, before He brings millions of dollars into your business, you will spend some nights on the winnowing floor!

Frustrations are not always caused by blatant sin or hidden sins. Often, the little foxes spoil the vines. Undesirable personality traits, personal feelings and opinions are like the chaff to the barley. In the grain, there is precious fruit the farmer has worked so hard to produce. Yet, the outside is a hard shell, the chaff, that must be broken off in order to yield the barley.

Likewise, the chaff in our lives must be broken off so that we can produce the fruit that God desires in our lives. The process of moving from blessing to blessing and climbing from 30-fold to 100-fold is connected to your ability to accept godly correction. Perhaps you will have to spend a night on the threshing floor. You may have to wrestle with an angel all night, as Jacob had to, or intercede all night in a garden, as Christ did!

Appointment With Destiny

Naomi understood what Ruth had to do and gave the young woman some life-changing instruction. Ruth's appointment with destiny had arrived. It was her time to get on the threshing floor.

> THEREFORE WASH YOURSELF AND ANOINT YOURSELF, PUT ON YOUR BEST GARMENT AND GO DOWN TO THE THRESHING FLOOR; BUT DO NOT MAKE YOURSELF KNOWN TO THE MAN UNTIL HE HAS FINISHED EATING AND DRINKING (RUTH 3:3).

Naomi understood men. To get a man's attention, don't distract him when his attention is focused on something else. There is a time to talk details and get down to business. Let the man finish his work for the day and eat a good meal. Men are more content after their bellies are full.

Herod had a feast and was having such a good time he gave a woman the head of John the Baptist on a silver plate! When a man is content and happy, he will give a woman just about anything she wants.

The Bible says that a woman from Lebanon came to Jesus, requesting prayer for her daughter. Because of her Gentile nationality, Christ refused to hear her. She appealed to the disciples, and was rejected by them, as well. Jesus went so far as to tell her He couldn't give the children's bread to the dogs.

Despite these setbacks, the woman began to worship the Lord (Matthew 15:21-28). Worship gets God's attention! The Lord is still seeking those who will worship Him (John 4:23).

She replied, "Yes, Lord, yet even the little dogs eat the crumbs which fall from their masters' table!" She was saying, "I may be a Gentile dog, but I don't need the whole loaf. All I need is a crumb from the Master's table!" She knew that the substance of the whole loaf could be found in the crumbs as well.

Her words moved Jesus! Remember, faith can be heard in WHAT you say! Some people go to the Lord in prayer and immediately say, "Help! I want. Give me and give us." Jesus began prayer by bragging on His Father. "Our Father in heaven, hallowed be Your name" (Matthew 6:9). Worship is the gateway to the heart of God.

God moves toward us when we minister to Him. As the worship of the Syro-Phoenician woman moved the heart of Jesus, He immediately moved to help the woman's daughter. Likewise, a man will move heaven and earth to help the woman he loves, when she brags on him!

The Bible said that "Boaz had eaten and drunk, and his heart was cheerful" (Ruth 3:7). Ruth was instructed to make her move after Boaz had cleared his mind from the day's work and had eaten a good meal. Naomi told Ruth to wash herself. She had to look her best. She wasn't to go to Boaz smelling like a grain silo, but to approach him in a feminine manner.

Ruth was a worker but was also a young lady. She was all woman. If Boaz was attracted to Ruth in the field, he would be more impressed when she was dressed up and looking like a lady! Naomi then said, "Get thee down to the floor" (Ruth 3:3). This is where the breakthrough comes—when we get to the floor on our knees in prayer, and spend time with our heavenly Boaz!

GET DOWN ON THE FLOOR

It was time to get down to business, down to where the rubber meets the road. This was the hour of decision. This was the time for divine reversal. It was the moment both Naomi and Ruth needed in order to change their destiny. Boaz was the man to do it.

Yet, in order to receive a complete hundred-fold blessing, you have to spend time with Boaz on the floor. This is not intended to sound crude or carnal. In the spiritual application, spending time on the floor is spending time in deep intimate prayer and worship before the Lord.

Ruth had known Boaz as a stranger, then as the boss of her workplace, and as a unique friend. Spurred on by Naomi, Ruth was now moving the relationship to another level.

Naomi gave Ruth explicit instructions about what to do when she entered Boaz's presence. Specifically, she told her that she was to mark the spot where Boaz lay.

On this particular night, Boaz chose to lie down for the night near a pile of grain. In ancient Israel, the enemy would often invade the land after the grain was at the threshing floor. The Philistines watched the Hebrews till the ground, plant the seed, water the soil, pull out the weeds, then harvest the barley and wheat.

Then, when the Hebrews took the grain to the threshing floor, the enemy would steal the grain, thus robbing the farmer of his increase and his finances. Remember, the Devil never plays by the rules. He comes "to steal, and to kill, and to destroy" (John 10:10). The enemy will let you pray, plant the seed, and get to the brink of your harvest, then suddenly bring a problem that will eat your finances and steal the blessing you have been waiting for.

The threshing floor is a place of battle. Boaz was sleeping near the pile of grain in order to protect it from any invader that might come at night! By Ruth coming to the floor, she was showing him again that as he protected the grain, she was willing to be by his side! The battle at the threshing floor turned into the blessing at the threshing floor.

THE TIME OF TESTING

Christ revealed to Peter that "Satan has asked for you, that he may sift you as wheat" (Luke 22:31). Jesus said Satan wanted to sift Peter's faith (Luke 22:32). All spiritual testing is designed to sift your faith. God sends a test to build your faith and character, but Satan sends a test to destroy your faith in God.

Satan told God that if He pulled the rug out from under Job and took his financial blessing, Job would lose his faith and curse God. When Job lost his wealth and his children, his wife encouraged him to curse God but he continued in his faith (Job 2:9).

When the test comes at the threshing floor, Satan intends to come and rob you of your blessing, wrecking your confidence in God's provision. On the other hand, God may allow the test to remove the chaff from your spirit and instill character in your life!

Peter's time of testing came BEFORE he was used to head the Jewish church in Jerusalem. Job's testing came PRIOR to his "double portion blessing" in Job 42:10. Ruth had to be steadfast and faithful, THEN the Lord brought her to the floor of Boaz.

> THEN IT SHALL BE, WHEN HE LIES DOWN, THAT YOU SHALL NOTICE THE PLACE WHERE HE LIES; AND YOU SHALL GO IN, UNCOVER HIS FEET, AND LIE DOWN; AND HE WILL TELL YOU WHAT YOU SHOULD DO (RUTH 3:4).

UNCOVERING THE FEET OF BOAZ

Naomi predicted that when Ruth "uncovered the feet" of Boaz, he would tell her what to do. There is something about the feet that is special to God. Feet that carry the good news of the gospel are blessed (Isaiah 52:7, Romans 10:15)! A woman broke open an alabaster box and washed Jesus' feet with her tears (Luke 7:38).

A New Testament word for worship means to "kiss toward." In one instance, where David speaks of worship, the word means to "bow toward." Worship involves a mental and physical prostration before God. When John saw the vision of Christ in Revelation 1:17, he "fell at his feet as one dead." In the four gospels, people who needed a miracle would fall at the feet of Jesus!

It was customary in the Middle East for a guest to remove his shoes when he entered the house, and the woman of the house would bring a basin and wash his feet. To exemplify the need for humility in a believer's life, Jesus, the Creator of the universe, washed the feet of His disciples. To wash someone's feet, one must bend down in an act of humility.

The time has come to return to some all-night prayer meetings, where we lie on the floor in the presence of God, worshiping at His feet. If we do so, we can arise from the floor knowing we have been changed!

We could call it a "Jacob encounter". The old patriarch didn't like what he saw in himself. So he wrestled an angel until sunrise. By the time it was over, he had a new name and a different walk. It's time to get down on the threshing floor with Boaz.

It Came To Pass At Midnight

Midnight is the turning point. Changes occur at midnight! The death angel came into Egypt at midnight (Exodus 12). Paul and Silas sang at midnight until the walls of the prison were shaken to the ground (Acts 16:25).

As darkness settled over Bethlehem and the full moon hung over the rugged Judean mountains, Ruth quietly made her way toward the threshing floor. As she stealthily approached Boaz, she knelt and uncovered his feet. It appears he didn't realize she was there for some time. Have you prayed and felt like God was paying you no attention?

> NOW IT HAPPENED AT MIDNIGHT THAT THE MAN WAS STARTLED, AND TURNED HIMSELF; AND THERE, A WOMAN WAS LYING AT HIS FEET. AND HE SAID, "WHO ARE YOU?" SO SHE ANSWERED, "I AM RUTH, YOUR MAIDSERVANT. TAKE YOUR MAIDSERVANT UNDER YOUR WING, FOR YOU ARE A CLOSE RELATIVE" (RUTH 3:8, 9).

As Ruth lay at his feet, Boaz spoke a blessing over her:

> THEN HE SAID, "BLESSED ARE YOU OF THE LORD, MY DAUGHTER! FOR YOU HAVE SHOWN MORE KINDNESS AT THE END THAN AT THE BEGINNING, IN THAT YOU DID NOT GO AFTER YOUNG MEN, WHETHER POOR OR RICH" (RUTH 3:10).

Boaz described Ruth as a virtuous woman. Because of her obedience and dedication, she received two blessings. First, Boaz announced he would perform the rite of the kinsman-redeemer. Then she received another unexpected blessing.

> SO SHE LAY AT HIS FEET UNTIL MORNING, AND SHE AROSE BEFORE ONE COULD RECOGNIZE ANOTHER. THEN HE SAID, "DO NOT LET IT BE KNOWN THAT THE WOMAN CAME TO THE THRESHING FLOOR." ALSO HE SAID, "BRING THE SHAWL THAT IS ON YOU AND HOLD IT." AND WHEN SHE HELD IT, HE MEASURED SIX EPHAHS OF BARLEY, AND LAID IT ON HER. THEN SHE WENT INTO THE CITY (RUTH 3:14, 15).

If we pray and labor in private, we will be rewarded openly. Ruth's story bears this out. Ruth began her labor in a small corner of the field. She then progressed to "handfuls on purpose." Ultimately she went home betrothed to Boaz and her veil overflowing with grain!

Boaz had decided that the time had come to "lay it on her". It was time to honor this woman for her obedience to God! This reminds me of the verse in Luke which says:

> GIVE, AND IT WILL BE GIVEN TO YOU: GOOD MEASURE, PRESSED DOWN, SHAKEN TOGETHER, AND RUNNING OVER WILL BE PUT INTO YOUR BOSOM. FOR WITH THE SAME MEASURE THAT YOU USE, IT WILL BE MEASURED BACK TO YOU (LUKE 6:38).

- ❏ Good measure is the 30-fold level.
- ❏ Pressed down and shaken together is the 60-fold level.
- ❏ Running over is the 100-fold level.

Ruth went from "just enough" to "enough and then some" and finally to the level of "more than enough". God brought increase! Because of Ruth's encounter with Boaz, he then performed the rite of the kinsman redeemer!

THE KINSMAN REDEEMER

If a husband died and there were no men in the family to inherit his land, the woman was to marry the brother of her husband in order to carry on the family name. If there were no brothers, then a next of kin could marry the woman and redeem the family inheritance. Since Boaz was a near kinsman, he had the right to redeem the land that belonged to Elimelech and Naomi.

Boaz called a meeting at the city gate and informed the people that if no one else was going to redeem the property of Elimelech, he would. As it turned out, there was a kinsman who was a closer relative than Boaz, but he was not willing to marry Ruth. This relative deferred to Boaz, who was more than willing to marry her. To legally close the deal, at the gate of the city, Boaz exchanged shoes with the other kinsman.

Chapter 7

When God Gets in your Shoes

Now this was the custom in former times in Israel concerning redeeming and exchanging, to confirm anything: one man took off his sandal and gave it to the other, and this was a confirmation in Israel (Ruth 4:7).

The exchanging of shoes meant, "Now I have a right to walk where I haven't walked before. I have legal authority to step into territory that I couldn't before!" Years before this, God had told Moses to remove the shoes from off his feet (Exodus 3:5). The ground was holy, God said. Therefore, out of respect, Moses removed his shoes.

Years ago I saw another reason why Moses removed his shoes. The job God had for Moses was too big for one man.

God was saying, "Moses, get your shoes off and let Me get in them! Let Me walk in your shoes down to Egypt!" Over 40 years later, God told Joshua to remove the "shoe" from off his foot. Notice that God said *shoe*, not *shoes*.

Take your sandal off your foot (Joshua 5:15).

Joshua knew the ground was holy, and that the "Commander of the army of the Lord" was in town to bring the walls of Jericho down (Joshua 5:14). If we understand the law of exchanging a shoe, God was saying,:

Joshua, I am about to give you this land. I am redeeming back this land for my people. Give me your shoe and I will give you the authority to walk through the land and to claim it for your people.

We need for God to get in our shoes. At times, things we attempt to accomplish are bigger than we are. They are bigger than our ability, bigger than our budget and bigger than our faith! When we let God take over the situation, and we declare, "The walls are bigger than I am able to scale and the enemy is stronger than I," then God can go with us and defeat the enemy!

From a Pauper to a Princess

As Boaz exchanged shoes, Ruth and Naomi experienced their biggest breakthrough in about 10 years! The land that was lost was restored. Something of great value had been redeemed! Once God gets in your shoes, your circumstances will change.

Once Boaz married Ruth, she was exalted to a position of prominence. Instantly, the entire city knew who this woman was. Suddenly, the men and women alike were pronouncing prophetic blessings on her life! The inhabitants proclaimed:

THE LORD MAKE THE WOMAN WHO IS COMING TO YOUR HOUSE LIKE RACHEL AND LEAH . . . AND MAY YOU PROSPER IN EPHRATHAH AND BE FAMOUS IN BETHLEHEM (RUTH 4:11, 12).

The greatest blessing was: *be famous in Bethlehem*! The people realized this marriage was not your normal "I-need-a-wife" and "I'm-after-a husband" relationship. Ruth didn't choose Boaz by chasing him across the barley field. She did not pursue him in romance nor flirt with him by bragging on his appearance. She just worked in the harvest. She kept her focus on the work and GOD brought in the man!

In her exaltation, she never forgot Naomi. In fact, she stayed connected to Naomi in a personal, intimate way. When her son, Obed, was born, it was Naomi who took the child and became its nurse. No, Naomi didn't get another son for Ruth to marry, but she did get a child of destiny to raise.

As Obed grew, perhaps Naomi told the child the story of the journey from Moab to Bethlehem, of God's provision and his mother's destiny. Naomi had quite a heritage to pass on to her grandson and, for that matter, to the world. If Naomi had written a book, perhaps it would have been called, *From Moab to Bethlehem — My Recovery from Tragedy.*

You must never forget the people who brought you to your position of success in your field. Was it a mother or father who helped you through school? Was it your wife or husband who believed in you when nobody else did? Did a pastor continue to encourage you, when others said you would never make it?

Was it a kingdom connection God sent to connect you with other people? Never forget from where He brought you. Don't dwell on the past but always appreciate those who pulled you out of Moab (the past) and brought you into the place of blessing!

How Prophecy Came to Pass

The inhabitants of Bethlehem spoke a prophetic word over Ruth and Boaz. They declared that their names would be famous in Bethlehem and in Ephratah. When reading the first few verses in Ruth, we see death, separation and sorrow. When we read the last few verses in the same book, we see victory, success and life.

The Bible says that Boaz and Ruth had a son named Obed. Obed had a son named Jesse, and Jesse had a son named David (Ruth 4:20-22). This is the same David that, many years later, was anointed to be king over all of Israel, and the same David to whom the promise of the Messiah was given.

David, the youngest of Jesse's sons, was a shepherd. Shepherd or not, this young man was destined for greatness. God's eye was on him from his mother's womb. David, like Ruth, took his assignment seriously.

As a shepherd, he challenged bears and lions in private battles on the rugged hillsides of Bethlehem. David was a man after God's own heart. Just like his ancestor, Ruth, he was a simple person with a deep purpose. He faithfully tended his father's sheep.

When Samuel was to anoint a king of Israel, he went by divine leading to Jesse's house. Seven of Jesse's sons were present, each hoping to be the chosen monarch. When Samuel the prophet passed, each boy inhaled and stuck out his chest. They had put on their best clothes and finest cologne. After God rejected all seven sons, Samuel asked, "Is there another boy?" Jesse said, "Yes but he's watching sheep."

God takes shepherds and makes them kings! If they can care for a flock and defend sheep with their own lives, then they will defend the people of God with their lives, if necessary.

David came out of the field with his staff in one hand, a slingshot in his hip pocket, and smelling like a cow pasture. Grass stains were on his backside and his fingernails were dirty from pulling up the poison grass that could make his sheep sick. Shocked and amazed, Jesse's seven sons stood back as Samuel anointed a teenage boy to be the next king of Israel! Though his great grandmother was a Moabite; though his family knew past sorrow and pain, God chose him to be the King of Israel.

You see, not only was his family heritage tainted with sorrow, but it was also marked with divine appointment and divine assignments. When Ruth came to Bethlehem, God had a little boy named David in mind!

When trouble comes to you in your Moab, and God moves you across the Jordan, remember that He seldom has just you in mind. We may never understand, in this life, why trouble and tragedy come to good people. Why does God allow famine and death? But if we can hold out long enough, we will discover that God has a plan that extends beyond our limited vision.

God Plans Long-Term Blessings

How many times does God pronounce a blessing upon your "seed" and your "seed's seed," or your children and your children's children? How often did the Lord say, in the Old Testament, for men to build an altar or monument where great spiritual events had transpired?

How many times did the Lord instruct them to tell the story to their children and their children's children?

When God blesses you, He seldom has only you in mind. He is thinking of future generations—ones you may never see.

This principle is clear in Hebrews, where the writer speaks of Abraham meeting Melchizedek, the priest of God. We read that Abraham paid tithe while Levi was still in his loins (Hebrews 7:9, 10). This illustrates how the blessings of God can continue for many generations!

SEVEN PRINCIPLES I HAVE LEARNED

After 28 years of ministry, I have learned seven great principles that agree with the same principles Ruth discovered as she moved into the blessing and favor of God!

One man said, "College gives you knowledge, but God gives you wisdom." Some things are best learned through practical experience. As we learn from our experiences, we need to ask God for wisdom so that we may pass along His truth to others who may encounter comparable situations. With this in mind, I want to share with you these seven spiritual truths which have been some of the foundational principles of our ministry!

❑ YOU MUST ENTER LITTLE DOORS BEFORE YOU CAN ENTER LARGE ONES

I have heard men preach and young people sing who can out-preach and out-sing most of the ministry personalities appearing on national Christian television. Often I have commented to Pam, "I wonder why they are not known on a national level."

It seems for many, it takes years for some to develop a ministry gift that is recognized. I believe the answer has to do with private battles. God raises up champions, not among champions, but among the sheep.

Moses was a shepherd before he was a pastor to three million people. David killed bears and lions in private before he defeated Goliath. When men can win private battles, God allows them to win public battles.

Some years ago, a great woman minister was destined, I believe, to be one of the most outstanding ministers in the nation. I often wondered why she never received national recognition. After years of marriage, she fell into adultery, lost her husband and, for several years, her ministry. What if she had been well known? The devastation within the body of Christ would have been great. God restrained her from becoming internationally known, to avoid another tragedy in the body of Christ.

Success can make or break a person. So God desires to build character in the minister before He builds the ministry. Are you becoming weary in thinking, "God is never going to use me?" Do you wonder why your gift has not been noticed? Are you sitting around waiting for a big door to open; or are you willing to do little things that no one notices? Are you willing to clean the church after service? Will you clean the bathrooms and sweep the sidewalk? Do you love God's house? Do you love God's people? Can you feel their needs and their hurts? God opens big doors when we are ready. If a big door has not opened, it may be that you are not as ready as you think!

❑ GOD USES PEOPLE TO GIVE INTO YOUR BOSOM

The Bible says that men shall "give into your bosom." The Bible says that Jesus found favor with both God and man (Luke 2:52)! God has always used men to bless men. The source is the Lord, but the method He uses to channel these blessings is men.

When a person is first called into the ministry, only a few churches desire to use him or her. Since he or she has little ministry experience, ministers are hesitant to use a person they may not know. I used to say, "How can I get the experience if they never use me?" This is where total dependency on God comes in. If I am called of God, then GOD will open the doors and He will speak to people to do it.

Early in our ministry, revivals began continuing for several weeks. Soon, the word spread and pastors were calling and requesting that I come to their churches and lead a revival. Not all of them were effective, but God moved on men to give us a door of opportunity for ministry. God can give you favor at work or on the job. He can speak to men and women to help open the door.

❑ NOT ALL OPEN DOORS ARE FROM GOD

God gives a person a vision. To distract you, Satan often gives you another vision. Something with two visions is a di-vision. A God-called evangelist should never try to pastor and a pastor should never try to evangelize. Each person has his gift and calling.

Sometimes a person will prophesy (or proph-a-lie) over a person, and declare the will of God for him or her. People often rely more on the words of a prophecy than they do on the instruction given in the Bible. I have met scores of people whose lives have been shattered and their families ruined because of a personal prophecy. A personal word from God will agree with and confirm what the Lord has already shown you.

When pressure is on, some desire to escape by discovering God's will somewhere else. When another apparent door opens, however, some assume that *this* is God's direction. Pastors change churches because there is contention in their congregation. They move, only to discover the same problems are waiting for them at the new church. The reason? People are people, sheep are sheep, and sheep always leave dung in the field.

❏ A Kingdom Connection Is Looking for You

God allows people to bless people. The Bible says men [shall] give into your bosom." Pastors open their churches and invite evangelists to speak. Thriving businesses are dependent on customers. Someone somewhere has an answer that you have been praying for. Out there somewhere is the person who holds the solution to your situation.

God connects people—Elijah and Elisha, Paul and Timothy, Elisha and the widow. God connects people for a purpose. My friend, Jentezen Franklin, calls these persons "kingdom connections."

In ages past, God has used widows to feed hungry prophets (2 Kings 4). During Christ's earthly tenure, God used several women with wealthy husbands to help finance His ministry

(Luke 8:1-2). Boaz was the miracle connection for two lonely widows who needed a financial and material breakthrough in their lives. There are thousands of Ruths in the church who are looking for a Boaz and thousands of Boazs looking for Ruths. This is why you must be in the right place at the right time and connected with the right people at the right season.

❏   THE TIMING OF GOD REVEALS THE PLAN OF GOD

You must be at the right place at the right time for the plan of God to be revealed to you. Timing may be the greatest key to the fulfilling of God's purposes.

The timing of God is a Kingdom key. God's timing may not always be our timing. We may speak about what the Lord has revealed to us concerning our future, but we may be speaking prematurely. What God has spoken to us may be years in advance of the actual fulfillment. Often, we are not ready for the very things we are believing about.

I've seen people hurt by unfaithful spouses. The person becomes lonely and enters a quick "let's-get-married" relationship. After several months, trouble brews as deep hidden emotions begin to boil to the surface. In such cases, the person has entered a relationship expecting someone to make them complete when they were not emotionally whole to begin with.

Here again, we see how important timing really is. You may not be ready for the very things you are praying about. God has a perfect time to launch your ministry and to bless your business and family.

Our ministry has been in six different buildings over the past 28 years. We have grown from one room in a small apartment to two large buildings totaling 75,000 square feet of space. Every time we ran out of room, I would go looking for another place. Every time I became frustrated, unable to find what we needed. Then, when I released my plans and turned them over to God, within a few days the unexpected always happened—we found the perfect place.

Had Ruth and Naomi not gone to Bethlehem at HARVEST TIME, they would have missed the immediate blessing and would not have fulfilled their destiny. If Ruth's destiny had not been fulfilled, God's plan for Israel's future would have been interrupted.

❏ OBEDIENCE RELEASES THE BLESSING

Obedience is simply "doing the Word of God." James said, "Faith without works is dead" (James 2:20). We would say, "Faith without corresponding action is dead." Your actions should correspond with what you believe.

Jesus often required ACTION before He actually healed a person. He would say, "Go show yourself to the priest," or "Rise, take up your bed and walk," or "Stretch forth your hand." When we act on what we believe, it is visible evidence that we actually do believe.

When a group of men tore off the roof and lowered a paralyzed man into the living room of a house where Jesus ministered, the Bible says, "Jesus SAW their faith" (Mark 2:5). God can see your faith when you act on His Word. This is true in relation to giving. When a minister receives the tithe and offerings, what do you hear and what is your reaction?

- ❏ ALL HE WANTS IS MY MONEY.
- ❏ I WISH HE WOULD HURRY UP SO WE COULD GET ON WITH CHURCH.
- ❏ ALL PREACHERS DO IS BEG FOR FINANCES.

The offering is my opportunity to sow my seed and reap a harvest. Can you imagine a farmer looking at the cold, dark ground and saying, "All that ground wants is my seed?" Or, "I'll just pass over this ground so I can get to my barn?" Or "All people want from farmers is food?"

If all you ever hear is MONEY when the offerings are received, then you need to clean out your ears. It is all about OBEDIENCE! Salvation comes through obedience; healing comes through obedience. In fact, ALL spiritual blessings come through obedience to God. If you are waiting for a giant door to open, think again. Little doors open first; after you walk through them, you will see more open doors. Ruth had to listen to the words of Boaz and obey them in order to obtain the blessing.

❏ A RHYTHM OF BLESSING FOLLOWS FAVOR AND OBEDIENCE

After years of faithfulness in your field of labor, there is a rhythm of blessing that you can encounter. Often you feel you are always planting seed and giving of yourself. The ultimate breakthrough seems impossible. Don't be discouraged.

In the Bible a Shunemite woman, after years of struggle, finally tapped into the rhythm of blessing. She and her husband prepared a chamber for the prophet Elijah. It was a place for him to spend the night as he traveled from "revival" to revival (2 Kings 4:8-10). As a result, she received five major miracles in her life.

- ❏ ALTHOUGH SHE WAS PHYSICALLY BARREN, GOD GAVE HER A SON (2 KINGS 4:14-17).

- ❏ HER SON DIED BUT GOD RAISED HIM FROM THE DEAD (2 KINGS 4:20-37).

- ❏ SHE WAS WARNED OF A SEVEN-YEAR FAMINE, AND WAS PROTECTED FROM THE DEVASTATION DURING THE FAMINE (2 KINGS 8:1, 2).

- ❏ SHE STOOD BEFORE THE KING SEVEN YEARS LATER TO PLEAD FOR HER LAND, AND THE KING RETURNED HER PROPERTY TO HER (2 KINGS 8:5, 6).

- ❏ SHE WAS GIVEN ALL THE FRUIT OF THE FIELD FOR A TOTAL OF SEVEN YEARS (2 KINGS 8:6).

I believe these blessings followed her because she prepared a place for the prophet of God. She sought first the kingdom of God, and as a result, many things were added to her.

There will come a time, as you are obedient to all the Lord commands you to do, that you will begin to see small doors open and little breakthroughs occur. Never criticize someone else's breakthrough or financial blessing, because you don't know what they have had to sow in order to receive those blessings.

I have met people who were worth millions of dollars. Some of these people relate how badly others envy them and become critical of them. Yet, when I hear their stories, I realize that those critical people are probably not willing to be as obedient as these people have been.

Some of these blessed people started out with nothing. Some were living in their cars or in small dilapidated houses. Because of their obedience and their sacrificial giving, however, God gave them a breakthrough in their finances. Their gift to the church, in return, is the gift of giving.

Remember, everyone starts in a corner. It may be a small church, a small ministry, a small business or a small checking account, but as you draw close to your Boaz (Jesus), and as you obey Him, He will send great favor and blessing into your life.

In Closing

The story of Ruth, Naomi and Boaz yields an enormous amount of practical information for our lives. In the pages of this book, I hope you have found an encouraging word, a nugget of truth that you can use in your life, or a challenge to apply Ruth's example to your life.

If you will commit yourself to the standards this young woman displayed in her life, and if you obey the words of our heavenly Boaz, Jesus, you will find that you will be living in the favor and blessing of God.

You too, will one day be able to say to Him, "Lay it on me."